Editor
Eric Migliaccio

Managing Editor
Ina Massler Levin, M.A.

Editor-in-Chief
Sharon Coan, M.S. Ed.

Illustrators
Victoria Frazier
Kevin Barnes

Cover Artist
Wendy Roy

Art Coordinator
Kevin Barnes

Creative Director
CJae Froshay

Imaging
James Edward Grace
Rosa C. See

Product Manager
Phil Garcia

Publisher
Mary D. Smith, M.S. Ed.

HOLIDAY BRAIN TEASERS

Grades 3-5

D1573158

Written by

Beth Thompson Fore

Teacher Created Resources, Inc.
6421 Industry Way
Westminster, CA 92683
www.teachercreated.com

ISBN: 978-0-7439-3351-3

©2001 Teacher Created Resources, Inc.
Reprinted, 2007
Made in U.S.A.

Table of Contents

Introduction

The activities in this book include hink pinks, quotation puzzles, math problems, and logic puzzles. These activities are designed to utilize higher-level thinking skills that encourage vocabulary usage, deductive reasoning, and problem-solving skills in enjoyable activities designed with a holiday theme.

Hink Pinks are words that rhyme. They can be one-syllable, two-syllable, or multi-syllable. Sometimes the solutions have a different number of syllables for each word. For example: a "thin colonist" would be a "slim pilgrim." The first word has one syllable and the second word has two syllables. In such cases, the number of syllables will be given in parentheses. Encourage students to use the dictionary, thesaurus, and any other helpful resources to assist them.

Quotation Puzzles encourage students to decode information and place letters together to make words and a meaningful quotation. Look at the puzzle below.

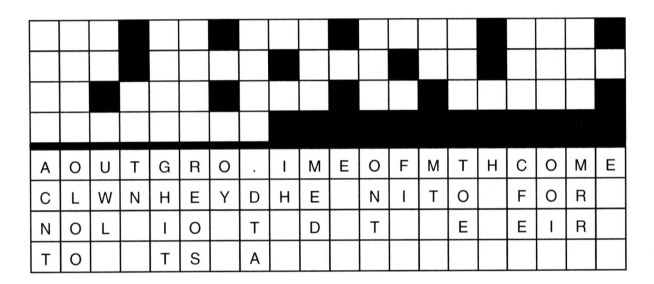

The fifth word has three letters. Look at the three columns under those spaces and try to make a 3-letter word by taking one letter from each column. The possibilities are "fir" and "for." Which one would most likely be in a sentence? The answer is "for." Write "for" in those blanks and mark the letters out in the columns below. Continue this process until you have a meaningful quote. In some places there is only one possible letter. The best way to approach the puzzle would usually be to decode the one- and two-letter words first. As letters are eliminated, it then becomes easier to decode the remaining letters.

(Answer to the puzzle: "Now is the time for all good men to come to the aid of their country.")

Math Problems require problem-solving skills. An understanding of simple measurements and fractions will also be helpful.

3

Introduction (cont.)

Logic Puzzles require students to use clues and match (O) items that fit together and eliminate (X) items that do not match. Some of the puzzles are single grid, some are double grid, and some are triple grid. Students use the information in the logic puzzles to deduce the correct answers. Occasionally, students will need to use a map, dictionary, encyclopedia, or other resource to assist them with factual information they do not know.

The purpose of logic puzzles is to encourage children to read information carefully and make logical deductions based on that information. Another important element of logic puzzles is to encourage children to write proof statements that support their conclusions. The proof statements can be abbreviated with symbols: = (equal); ≠ (not equal); ∴ (therefore). If a clue states that one thing does not match another, an X is placed on the matrix where the two items intersect. When a match is made and an O is placed on a matrix, the rest of that vertical column and horizontal row become Xs.

When a double or triple matrix is used, the individual matrices can be combined with other matrices to give additional information. In some of these logic puzzles, this combining of information is essential to the solution of the problem.

The teacher should work the first logic problem with the students and show them how to write the proof and combine clues. It is effective to use an overhead for this purpose. It is also a good idea to continue using the overhead with future logic puzzles and have students write proofs and explanations for the entire class to see. Look at the following example:

Four children went "trick-or-treating" on Halloween night. The children's names were George, Amy, Ralph, and Kelly. The children were dressed as a ghoul, Frankenstein, a vampire, and a mummy. Which child dressed in which costume?

Clues:
1. The ghoul and the vampire went "trick-or-treating" together.
2. When Ralph saw Kelly, he said, "You look batty in that costume."
3. Amy has never met Kelly.
4. George is never "frank" in anything he says or does.
5. George did not dress as a ghoul for Halloween.

	houl	Frankenstein	vampire	mummy
George	x	x	x	o
Kelly	x	x	o	x
Amy	x	o	x	x
Ralph	o	x	x	x

Proof:
#1 Kelly = vampire
#2 Amy ≠ ghoul
#3 George ≠ Frankenstein
#4 George ≠ ghoul
#5 ∴ George = mummy

Halloween Hink Pinks

Hink Pinks are pairs of one-syllable words that rhyme. Hinky Pinkies are pairs of two-syllable words that rhyme. Hinkity Pinkities are pairs of three-syllable words that rhyme. Use the clues below to decode these Halloween-related Hink Pinks.

Hink Pinks

1. a spirit's brag _____

2. an evil spirit's hammer and wrench _____

3. obese feline _____

4. a fearful evening _____

5. a winged night creature's headgear _____

Hinky Pinkies

1. a hag's trousers _____

2. limping ghost _____

3. bloodsucker's evening light_____

4. an embalmed body's card game _____

5. country person's jack-o'-lanterns _____

6. fine sweets _____

Hinkity Pinkities

1. a bony framework's jiggly dessert _____

2. a vampire's shoulder blades _____

Trick or Treat!

Four children went "trick-or-treating" on Halloween night. Each one had a favorite treat he or she was hoping to receive. Read the clues below to help you decide which treat belongs with which child.

Clues:

1. Tyler doesn't think receiving money on Halloween night is as good as getting candy; Bridget agrees.

2. Bobby doesn't have a "sweet tooth."

3. One year, Tyler left his Halloween treats near the fireplace for too long. Now, he doesn't like treats that melt easily.

4. Pam plans to build a birdhouse from all of the sticks left over from her favorite treat.

5. The children who share the same first letter of their first names don't like the taste of candy corn.

Favorite Treats

	chocolate	candy corn	money	lollipop
Bobby				
Bridget				
Pam				
Tyler				

Halloween Traditions

Match the following five countries with some of their Halloween customs—historical and contemporary—and with the objects sometimes associated with their customs.

Clues:

1. The country that houses Buckingham Palace was not known for using stones or torches in their Halloween rituals.

2. The people who paraded through the villages carrying torches to drive away evil spirits and witches were not from the country that houses the Statue of Liberty.

3. Americans use a pumpkin on Halloween, but they don't go around begging for food.

4. The Irish used the object that is commonly referred to today as the jack-o'-lantern, but they did not bob for apples or use regular pumpkins.

5. The country commonly associated with bagpipes did not bob for apples or use pumpkins.

6. The country whose name is a homonym for a word meaning "loud moans or howls" believed that everyone should place a stone into a bonfire. If the stone was missing the next morning, then he or she would die within a year.

7. The countries composing the United Kingdom do not have "trick-or-treating" as their custom.

	Objects						**Customs**			
	stones	pumpkins	apples	torches	jack-o'-lanterns	predicting death	trick-or-treating	begging for food	driving away evil spirits	bobbing for apples
England										
Wales										
Ireland										
United States										
Scotland										

Wilma Witch's Party

Wilma Witch is having a Halloween party. The problems in this exercise sometimes require information from a preceding problem. Have fun solving these problems!

1. Wilma Witch is stirring her famous brew. The following recipe is good for 10 guests. Wilma wants to know what the recipe would be for 25 guests. Help her out!

   Recipe
   - 20 bat tongues
   - 14 cat tails
   - 150 goblin toenails

   New Recipe
   - _____ bat tongues
   - _____ cat tails
   - _____ goblins' toenails

2. There are 3000 witches invited to Wilma's party. Half of the witches will attend the party. One-third of the witches will go to George Ghost's party. The rest of the witches plan to stay home and rest this Halloween. How many witches will stay home? _____

3. The witches who attend Wilma's party will play games. 500 will play "Ugly Face" cards and 394 will play "Spin the Broom." If the remaining witches play "Pin the Nose on the Ghost," how many will be playing that game? _____

4. The witches decide to make masks at Wilma's party. One-fifth of them make Frankenstein masks, two-fifths make beautiful princess masks, and the others make animal masks. How many witches will make each kind of mask?

   _____ Frankenstein masks

   _____ princess masks

   _____ animal masks

5. The witches divided into three groups to sing scary songs. How many witches were in each group if the groups were even? _____

6. Half of the witches attending Wilma's party live in the South Swamp, and half of them live in the North Swamp. It is 400 miles to Wilma's house from the South Swamp and 600 miles from the South Swamp to the North Swamp. Wilma's house is between the two swamps. The witches travel at 50 m.p.h. How long will it take each group of witches to reach Wilma's house?

South Swamp
_____

North Swamp
_____

Halloween Trick-or-Treaters

Six children—three boys and three girls—went trick-or-treating together on Halloween night. Then they returned to Dena's house to play games and enjoy some of their treats. Match the children with their costumes and write their names and costumes in the proper location around the table. Each child is sitting facing the table. (First, you will need to identify the names of the six children and the costumes they wore. Be sure you read carefully when the clues tell you left and right!)

Clues:

1. The hostess sat at the head of the table, but she didn't masquerade as a ghost or as Cinderella.

2. The mummy sat directly across from Sarah, but neither of them sat at the head of the table; however, they did sit on either side of the person disguised as "The Great Pumpkin."

3. Mark sat directly opposite Dena and to the immediate left of Laura.

4. Two girls sat side-by-side on one side of the table; neither of them dressed as a ghost.

5. Sean sat directly across from the vampire and to the immediate right of the mummy.

6. Philip sat directly across from Cinderella, but he did not sit beside Frankenstein.

Name: _____

Costume: _____

Name: _____

Costume: _____

Head of the Table

Name: _____

Costume: _____

Name: _____

Costume: _____

Name: _____

Costume: _____

Name: _____

Costume: _____

Halloween Word Search

```
S  A  G  K  P  M  U  P  C  O  S  T  U  M  E  E  R  F
G  K  N  H  M  A  G  M  Y  K  M  M  V  M  G  C  R  R
N  O  E  M  O  H  G  I  E  D  R  A  C  U  L  A  Y  I
I  I  Y  L  O  S  L  L  O  W  M  E  E  N  N  R  D  G
B  O  B  U  E  E  T  R  I  P  U  M  P  K  I  N  N  H
B  Y  L  B  T  T  E  H  I  H  I  S  E  O  B  I  A  A
O  M  A  O  A  L  O  R  G  R  P  N  E  O  B  V  C  U
B  M  N  C  N  B  E  N  B  I  S  A  R  B  O  A  R  N
C  U  T  R  I  C  K  O  R  T  R  E  A  T  H  L  T  T
A  M  E  I  C  K  P  I  E  R  F  F  R  O  G  E  R  E
C  T  R  A  H  C  T  I  W  R  F  R  A  N  K  E  R  D
C  A  N  D  I  O  N  E  E  W  O  L  L  A  H  L  L  I
```

bat	costume	Halloween	skeleton
bobbing	Dracula	haunted	spirit
brew	Frankenstein	lantern	trick or treat
candy	fright	mummy	vampire
carnival	ghost	pumpkin	witch
cat	ghoul		

Decode this message about witches!

Each letter below stands for a different letter in the alphabet. For starters, in this puzzle, every time you see the letter **N** you should write the letter **S** above it. (**Clue:** The second word is one of the 50 U.S. States.)

_ _ _ _ _ , _ _ _ _ _ _ _ _ _ _ _ _ _ , _ _ _

N Q G U V   V Q N N Q T O L N U C C N   W N   Q

_ _

C Z A X W X   Q V U F W T Q Q N N Z T W Q C U E

_ _ _ _   _ _ _ _ _ _ .

A W C O   A W C T O U N

Thanksgiving Dinner

Six cousins sit down at the table for their annual Thanksgiving feast. Each child has a favorite Thanksgiving food. Match each child with his/her favorite Thanksgiving food.

Clues:

1. The identical male twins do not like anything sweet.

2. The children whose names begin with the same letter do not consider meat their favorite food.

3. The oldest child prefers a "fowl" odor in the kitchen.

4. The twins are younger than Laura, who is not the eldest.

5. The youngest child loves dessert best.

6. Jeff is a clown at Thanksgiving dinner, and the others have nicknamed him after his favorite food.

7. Tara is neither the eldest nor the youngest; and she doesn't like sweets, meat, or dressing.

Favorite Food

	corn	ham	pumpkin pie	dressing	turkey	sweet yams
Jeff						
Tara						
Susie						
Lynne						
Laura						
Kyle						

Creating a Thanksgiving Day

Thanksgiving Day has not always been a holiday. Certain people initiated certain times to establish such a day, but the day has changed over the years. Use the following clues to help you decide which people initiated a certain day to celebrate Thanksgiving Day.

Clues:

1. The 16th president of the United States first declared the last Thursday of November as an official day, saying it was "a day of thanksgiving and praise to our beneficent Father."
2. The editor of *Godey's Lady's Book* promoted the idea of a National Thanksgiving Day. Her ideas influenced the president mentioned above.
3. The president who was a victim of polio and the initiator of the New Deal established the next-to-last Thursday of November as Thanksgiving. This helped businesses by lengthening the shopping period before Christmas.
4. The president with wooden teeth did not establish the fourth Thursday nor the last Thursday in November as Thanksgiving Day.
5. The legislative branch of the government declared Thanksgiving a legal federal holiday on the fourth Thursday in November.

	Event								**Date**		
	declared legal federal holiday	1st declared official day	help business	promoted National Thanksgiving Day	issued general proclamation	next-to-last Thursday in Nov.	4th Thursday in November	last Thursday in November	November 26th	National Thanksgiving
Lincoln										
Sarah Hale										
Congress										
Washington										
Roosevelt										

A Thanksgiving Feast

Eight people are gathered around the dining room table at Ralph and Mary Johnson's house for a Thanksgiving feast. Read the clues below and determine the name of the person sitting at each place and his/her favorite food.

Guest List	
Angie	Johnny
Ann	Mary
Bill	Ralph
Jeffrey	Susie

Food List	
corn	pie
dressing	potatoes
green beans	rolls
ham	turkey

1. Ralph is at the head of the table, and he doesn't like corn.

2. No male sits beside another male.

3. Angie and Jeffrey are brother and sister; Johnny and Susie are also brother and sister. Each brother and sister pair sits side-by-side on the same side of the table.

4. The person who likes ham sits to Ralph's right at the table.

5. Bill's wife, Ann, sits to his left at the table. Ralph's wife loves dressing.

6. Susie sits to Bill's right and across from the person who loves green beans. Susie loves bread.

7. Jeffrey is a meat lover, and he can't wait for the turkey to be carved.

8. Two males love pie and corn, and they sit across the table from each other.

Name: _____	Name: _____	Name: _____
Food: _____	Food: _____	Food: _____

Head of the Table

Name: _____
Food: _____

Name: _____
Food: _____

Name: _____	Name: _____	Name: _____
Food: _____	Food: _____	Food: _____

Thanksgiving Activities

Hink Pinks

Hink Pinks are pairs of rhyming words. Beside the clues below, the number of syllables in each word in the answer is shown in parentheses.

1. bird cry (1, 1)_____

2. pork jelly (1, 1) _____

3. purchase dessert (1, 1)_____

4. corn obsession (1, 1) _____

5. thin American colonist (1, 2) _____

6. colonists' ship's strength (3, 2) _____

"Thanksgiving" Words

Use the letters in the word "Thanksgiving" to make words consisting of four or more letters each. Place the words in the appropriate columns. Then add your total scores. (In each column, you may use the letters only as often as they appear in the word "Thanksgiving." For example, you may use two *i*s and two *g*s but only one *a*. Proper nouns are not allowed.)

4 letters (1 point)	5 letters (2 points)	6 letters (3 points)	7+ letters (4 points)

Thanksgiving Activities

Quotation Puzzle

Decode this quotation. The letters in column one will be placed in the blank squares in column one. The letters in column two will be placed in the blank squares in column two, etc. Words are separated by black boxes. It is easy to decode the quotation by first determining the short words (one to three letters), then the longer words. As letters are used, mark through them at the top so that the remaining letters will make it easier to decode the rest of the quotation.

D	A	E			D	A	A					V	E	R		B	H		A	E	
T	H	E		F	H	E	H	C				V	E	R		B	H		A	E	
T	H	G	E	I	I	L	I	E		P	O	C	E	L	E	T	I	A	E	E	D
T	O	O	S	T	N	R	R	T	E	S	H	L	G	R	I	M	R	R	I	N	D
T	O	Y	K	.	P	T	S	.	N	T	I	A	N	K	S	G	S	V	T	N	G

The Cost of Thanksgiving Dinner

Bill and Betty Thompson are hosting Thanksgiving dinner at their house this year. Consider the following information, and answer the questions about the cost and amount of food they will need in preparation for Thanksgiving dinner.

Eight adults and ten children will be present at the dinner. If every adult eats ⅓ of a pound of turkey, and every child eats ⅒ of a pound of turkey . . .

1. What is the least amount of turkey the Thompson's will need to feed everyone? _____

2. If the turkey costs $1.25 per pound, what is the least amount of money the turkey will cost to feed the Thompson family? _____

3. Betty Thompson has a recipe for a cheese squash casserole that serves six people. Beside the ingredients below, write the amount of each ingredient she will need to feed her guests.

Recipe for Six

- 6 cups sliced zucchini
- 2 beaten eggs
- 1 ⅓ cups sour cream
- 2 tablespoons all-purpose flour
- 2 stiffly beaten egg whites

- 1 ½ cups shredded cheese
- 6 slices bacon
- 1 tablespoon butter
- ¼ cup dry bread crumbs

Recipe for _____

- _____ cups sliced zucchini
  (a)
- _____ beaten eggs
  (b)
- _____ cups sour cream
  (c)
- _____ tablespoons all-purpose flour
  (d)
- _____ stiffly beaten egg whites
  (e)

- _____ cups shredded cheese
  (f)
- _____ slices bacon
  (g)
- _____ tablespoons butter
  (h)
- _____ cups dry bread crumbs
  (i)

4. The total cost of the Thanksgiving meal is $120. The children are responsible for 48% of the total cost of the meal.

   a. What is the total cost of the food for the children? _____

   b. What is the cost for each individual child? _____

   c. What is the total cost for the adults? _____

   d. What is the cost for each individual adult? _____

   e. The desserts account for ⅕ of the total cost. How much do the desserts cost?_____

Thanksgiving Word Search

```
T F A T I L Y R R E B N A R C Y A S
F H T H A N K A E B D A I Y A E S T
F E A A P I L P R B R U L K N K S N
G I A N I K L E A V M I T T P R M O
L G N S K P B B E R M E S I E U A R
N E N G T M O F E A M E V V T T Y D
I T A I E U B C F V V A R U A A S U
F U G V F P A S U R E A A R D P R O
F M O I E F T H A N K S G I V I N G
U N U N A S U H M I R I L O B E S P
T E R G O U R T A A A O G O U R D A
S U J O Y A D I S O H R C O R R I T
```

autumn	gratitude	pie
cornucopia	ham	pumpkin
cranberry	harvest	stuffing
family	holiday	Thansksgiving
feast	leaves	turkey
gourd	November	yams

Decode this Thanksgiving message!

Each letter below stands for a different letter in the alphabet. For starters, in this puzzle, every time you see the letter **M** you should write the letter **A** above it.

```
___ ___ ___ ___ ___ ___ ___ ___ ___ ___ ___ ___   ___ ___ ___   ___ ___   ___   ___ ___ ___ ___
 C   B   M   G   P   O   Q   R   X   R   G   Q      E   M   Z      R   O      M      C   R   A   K

___ ___ ___ ___   ___ ___ ___ ___   ___ ___ ___ ___ ___ ___ ___ ___ ___   ___ ___ ___ ___ ___ ___
 Y   B   K   G      A   M   G   Z      M   A   K   V   R   I   M   G   O      Q   M   C   B   K   V

___ ___ ___ ___   ___ ___ ___ ___ ___   ___ ___ ___ ___ ___ ___ ___ ___   ___ ___ ___
 Y   R   C   B      C   B   K   R   V      N   M   A   R   F   R   K   O      M   G   E

___ ___ ___ ___ ___   ___ ___ ___ ___ ___   ___ ___ ___ ___ ___ ___ ___ ___.
 I   D   W   G   C      C   B   K   R   V      J   F   K   O   O   R   G   Q   O
```

Christmas Critters

Two families are well-known at this winter season of the year: the Claus family and the Frostbite Snowman family. The members of these families are: Santa Claus, Mrs. Claus, DePendent Claus (their dependent son), Mr. Frostbite Snowman, and Mrs. Frostbite Snowman. Each member of each family owns his/her own reindeer named Comet, Cupid, Donner, Blitzen, or Rudolph. Each member of each family also has his/her own favorite drink: orange juice, hot chocolate, hot tea, soda, and milk.

Match each family member with his/her reindeer and favorite drink.

Clues:

1. Mr. Frostbite doesn't own the "reindeer of love" because Mr. Frostbite was once a happy bachelor.
2. DePendent Claus hates to drink any hot drink.
3. Santa Claus is such a football freak that he named his reindeer after a football play.
4. The ladies are partial to hot drinks.
5. The Claus family gets very upset with the Frostbites because one of their reindeer is always blowing his nose, which is always fiery-colored and shiny from the cold.
6. Mrs. Frostbite says that her reindeer is speedier than a scientific phenomenon—so she named him accordingly.
7. DePendent Claus likes carbonated beverages.
8. The tea lover owns Donner. The milk lover owns Rudolph.

	Drinks					Reindeer				
	orange juice	hot chocolate	hot tea	soda	milk	Comet	Cupid	Donner	Blitzen	Rudolph
Santa Claus										
Mrs. Claus										
DePendent Claus										
Mr. Frostbite										
Mrs. Frostbite										

Christmas Around the World

There are many ways of saying Merry Christmas: "Joyeux Noel," "Boun Natale," "Felices Pascuas," "Gledelig Jul," and "S Rozhdestvom Khristovym" are a few of them. There are also some unusual customs and foods in different countries around Christmas time. For instance, some children use shoes instead of stockings to hold their goodies; some people eat capitone (a large female eel) on Christmas Eve; some people use a spider web as a tree decoration to indicate good luck for the family; some eat Christmas pudding with an almond in it, and whoever gets the almond is the next to get married; and some dance the Jota on Christmas Eve. These sayings and customs come from the following five countries: Russia, Italy, France, Norway and Spain. Use the clues to help you determine how each country says Merry Christmas and one of their Christmas customs.

Clues:

1. The countries that say "Buon Natale" and "Felices Pascuas" instead of "Merry Christmas" are located between the north 30th and 50th parallels on the world map.
2. One of the Scandinavian countries says "Gledelig Jul" instead of Merry Christmas.
3. In Russia they do not eat capitone on Christmas Eve; nor do they enjoy Christmas pudding.
4. In Italy they do not dance the Jota or use shoes instead of stockings on Christmas Eve.
5. The countries bordered by the Arctic Ocean do not eat capitone or dance the Jota as part of their Christmas celebration.
6. The country that has historically and culturally influenced Mexico says "Felices Pascuas" instead of Merry Christmas.
7. The former communist country, which was a republic in the U.S.S.R., does not use shoes for stockings; nor does it say "Joyeux Noel."
8. The country that borders the North Sea believes that an almond in your Christmas pudding indicates that a person will soon be married.
9. The Parisians wish you "Joyeux Noel" and hope that your shoes may be filled with goodies on Christmas Eve.

	"Merry Christmas"					Tradition				
	Joyeux Noel	Buon Natale	Felices Pascuas	Gledelig Jul	S. Rozhdestvom Khristovym	shoes	capitone	spider web	Christmas pudding	Jota
Russia										
Italy										
France										
Norway										
Spain										

Santa's Gifts

Santa Claus has just arrived at the Carlson's house on Christmas Eve. He is placing Sarah and the other children's Christmas presents on the floor around him. Read the clues below and determine the name of each child and the present Santa has brought him/her.

Christmas List	
Ashli	Richard
Jeni	Sarah
Nick	Tim

Gift List	
baseball glove	sneakers
skateboard	stereo
skates	video game

1. The present that is furthest to Santa's left is Jeni's present, and she doesn't like anything athletic.

2. Santa brought one of the boys a stereo, which he is placing on his extreme right.

3. Tim's and Nick's presents are next to each other, but neither is next to Richard's or Jeni's gifts, and neither present is on the end.

4. Ashli's baseball glove is immediately between Jeni's present and the sneakers.

5. The skates and the skateboard are next to each other, but they are not next to the video game.

6. A girl is receiving the skateboard as a present, and her present is not located next to Nick's.

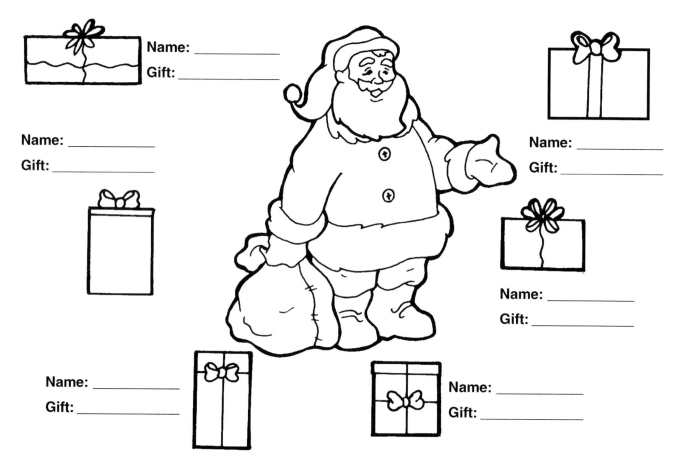

Name: _____
Gift: _____

Name: _____
Gift: _____

Name: _____
Gift: _____

Name: _____
Gift: _____

Name: _____
Gift: _____

Name: _____
Gift: _____

Christmas Concerns

1. If Santa Claus was born 100 years ago today, how many days old would he be today?

   _____

2. Santa plans to leave San Francisco at 6:00 P.M. on Christmas Eve. It will take him four hours to fly to Miami, Florida. What time and what day will he arrive in Miami?

   _____

3. Your mother gives you a choice of how many pieces of candy you would like to have in your Christmas stocking. Look at the following choices. Convert them into the decimal system, and choose the one that represents the most candy.

   a. CDLXIV pieces of candy = _____

   b. 39 dozen pieces of candy = _____

   c. 22^2 pieces of candy = _____

4. Rudolph flies three times as fast as Cupid, but only two-thirds as fast as Blitzen. If Cupid flies 320 miles in four hours, at what speed per hour do each of the three reindeer fly?

   Cupid = _____

   Rudolph = _____

   Blitzen = _____

5. Mrs. Claus is concerned about her weight. Last year she weighed ⅔ what she weighs this year. This year she weighs 1½ times what she weighed two years ago. If Mrs. Claus weighed 160 pounds last year, how much did she weigh two years ago and how much does she weigh this year?

   2 years ago = _____

   1 year ago = _____

   this year = _____

Christmas Word Search

```
C  A  R  O  L  S  N  S  T  N  E  S  E  R  P  N  A  C
T  H  Y  T  S  O  D  E  C  O  R  A  T  I  O  N  S  P
E  P  R  L  T  Y  A  D  I  L  O  H  G  E  I  L  R  O
S  L  E  I  G  H  T  F  S  N  O  W  M  A  N  E  E  C
N  O  I  G  S  F  R  S  L  E  G  H  I  R  S  X  B  C
I  D  N  H  O  T  C  H  O  C  O  L  A  T  E  E  M  A
O  U  D  T  N  O  M  A  P  R  I  T  A  S  T  E  E  N
P  R  E  S  A  N  T  A  N  E  F  R  D  A  T  R  C  D
A  L  E  S  N  I  T  Y  S  D  R  E  T  N  I  W  E  L
S  L  R  I  B  B  O  N  Y  T  I  V  I  T  A  N  D  E
```

candle	lights	Santa
carols	nativity	sleigh
Christmas	poinsettia	snowman
December	presents	star
decorations	reindeer	tinsel
frosty	ribbon	tree
holiday	Rudolph	winter
hot chocolate		

Decode this message about Christmas!

Each letter below stands for a different letter in the alphabet. For example, in this puzzle, every time you see the letter **E** you should write the letter **C** above it.

_ _ _ _ _ _ _ _ _ _ _ _ _ _ _ _ _ _ _ _ _ _ _ _ _ _ _

E Q H N L A O J L   N L   J V   W T E N A N V X   A N O W

_ _ _ _ _ _ _ _ _ _ _ _ _ _ _ _ _ _ _ _

B Y H   E Q N I U H W V   J A N O W   B N I I W U

_ _ _ _ _ _ _ _ _ _ _ _ _ _ _ _ _ _ _

R N A Q   K Y G   J V U W T E N A W O W V A !

Christmas Activities

Hink Pinks

Hink Pinks are two rhyming words. Beside the clues below, the number of syllables in each word in the answer is shown in parentheses.

1. Santa's teeth cleaner (1, 1) _____

2. inexpensive present (1, 1) _____

3. complimentary cedar (1, 1) _____

4. happy red-berry shrub (2, 2) _____

5. "joyful Christmas song" clothing (2, 2) _____

"Christmas" Words

Use the letters in the word "Christmas" to make words consisting of three or more letters each. Place the words in the appropriate columns. Then add your total scores. (You may use the letters only as often as they appear in the word "Christmas." For example, you may use the letter **s** twice but you may use the letter **a** only once in each word.) Do not use abbreviations or proper nouns.

3 letters (1 point)	4 letters (2 points)	5 letters (3 points)	6+ letters (4 points)

Santa's Christmas Route

You will need a map with longitude and latitude to complete this page.

It's almost Christmastime and Santa's on his way.

He'll visit each town and city by the arrival of Christmas Day.

He'll fly south to Europe to a major capital city.

When he arrives at 41° N, 13° E, he'll sing a Christmas ditty. _____
(1)

Then Santa will fly southeast over the _____ Canal,
(2)

And the sea he will cross over matches Rudolph, his reindeer pal _____.
(3)

He'll travel southwest across Africa to the Ivory Coast. "_____ is our
capital," is the natives' boast.   (4)

Then off to the southeast of Africa to a large offshore island.

"_____ is our destination," choruses his tiny reindeer band.
(5)

The reindeer change direction and fly north of the Tropic of Cancer.

"Let's fly over eastern Asia to Seoul, _____," says the feisty little
Prancer.   (6)

Momentarily, Prancer thinks a minute and scratches his tiny ear,

"If it's 1:00 P.M. in London, what time will it be here?" _____
(7)

Then Santa crosses southern Asia and goes to the country of _____,
to Bombay.   (8)

He crosses the _____ Mountains as he proceeds along this way.
(9)

He travels southeast to Singapore and wonders where he's at.

"Santa," shouts Cupid, "we're at _____ Long. and Lat!"
(10)

Then they dash across the sky like lightning and thunder.

They're headed southeast to _____, the land "down under."
(11)

Santa's Christmas Route *(cont.)*

They sing happy Christmas carols filled with joy and mirth,

And they make their way southwest across the continent to the main city of

_____.
　　　(12)

Then Santa's off to Alaska and needs the shortest route that's best.

Will he fly _____, or will he fly northwest?
　　　　　　　(13)

How many time zones does Santa cross en route to Anchorage? _____
　　　　　　　　　　　　　　　　　　　　　　　　　　　　　　　(14)

At least he won't have to worry if his perishables aren't stored in the fridge!

Santa travels east across the _____ Mountains to the capital of Canada.
　　　　　　　　　　　　　　　(15)

_____ Is the capital Toronto? Is it Montreal? Or is it Ottawa?
　　　(16)

Santa travels south toward the equator on the same meridian.

When he arrives in Colombia's capital, _____, he promises the
reindeer some fun!　　　　　　　　　　　　(17)

He travels south through the _____ Mountains,
　　　　　　　　　　　　　　　　　(18)

Then due east along the Tropic of Capricorn.

By the time they arrive across the continent in the farthest eastern coastal city of

_____,
　　　(19)

Santa's looking extremely tired and forlorn.

His last destination is _____,
and Santa can't　　　　　　　　(your home town)
quite figure it out,

So write at least four more lines
of rhyme and help Santa plan
his route!

Merry Christmas!

Valentine Gifts

Five boys wanted to show their affection for five girls, but each wanted to do so in his own way. Use the clues below to help you match the boys with their girlfriends and their Valentine gifts to them.

Clues:

1. Erin received a romantic valentine from her secret admirer, whose name did not begin with a letter in the last half of the alphabet; and it did not have the same number of letters as her own.

2. Steve is a practical joker, so he purchased a fake arachnid and slipped it inside his girlfriend's desk.

3. One boy, whose girlfriend shares his first initial, thinks she is sweet; so he gave her a sweet edible surprise.

4. Sean has a good sense of humor and hates "mushy" gifts, so he sent his girlfriend a humorous surprise through the mail.

5. Lisa has stickers all over her notebook, so her boyfriend (whose name doesn't begin with "C") gave her one as a gift.

6. Monica nearly jumped out of her skin and screamed loudly from fright when she received her gift; while the candy recipient replied excitedly, "Oh, John, you really shouldn't have!"

	Erin	Lisa	Cathy	Monica	Jennifer	sticker	funny valentine	candy	spider	romantic valentine
John										
Sean										
Chris										
Steve										
Jason										

Recipient   **Gift**

Valentine's Day Customs

There are various customs and forms of celebrations that occur in different countries on Valentine's Day. Some countries make and exchange valentine cards. One country sends snowdrops (pressed flowers) or gaekkebrevs (joking letters signed by dots). If the recipient of the letter guesses the sender, she receives an Easter egg on Easter. Another country bakes Valentine buns with caraway seeds, plums, or raisins. Still another country holds a Valentine's feast.

Use the clues to help you determine the various customs of each of the following countries: England, Denmark, Italy, and Canada.

Clues:

1. The North American countries do not send snowdrops nor gaekkebrevs on Valentine's Day.

2. In the country where the Ancient Romans lived, some women rise before sunrise and stand at their window watching for a man to pass. They believe that the first man they see, or someone who looks like him, will marry them within a year.

3. The North American country with a large French-speaking population uses stamps for their Valentine's celebration.

4. A Valentine's Feast is not held in the country where the Thames River flows.

5. The Scandinavian country does not use food as a part of its Valentine's Day celebration.

	gaekkebrevs	Valentine Cards	Valentine Buns	Valentine Feast
England				
Denmark				
Italy				
Canada				

The Valentine's Dance

Ten high-school students—including Ted, Ben, and Shawn—are attending the Valentine's Dance. Each couple is waiting in line to have their picture taken in front of the life-size valentine. Use the clues below to determine which boys and girls are together at the dance and where each couple is in the line.

Clues:

1. Jason and Heather are neither first nor last in line, and they are not a couple.

2. Jennifer and John are first and fifth in line, respectively; their dates are Ben and Angie.

3. Heather is in line between her two best friends, Kelly and Julie, neither of whom is at the dance with Shawn.

4. The couple who shares the same first letter of their names is next to the last couple in line, and they are in front of Angie.

1st: _____

_____

2nd: _____

_____

3rd: _____

_____

5th: _____

_____

4th: _____

_____

Valentine's Day Math

1. Melanie has purchased five special valentines that she wants to give to her close friends and family. The cards cost $1.25, $1.75, $2.00, $1.65, and $2.50. She also plans to give away two boxes of candy: one costs $6.95 and the other costs $3.50.

   a. How much money will Melanie spend for Valentine's Day? _____

   b. Melanie has $25.00 in her piggy bank at home and $100.00 in the bank. Will she need to take some money out of the bank? If so, how much? _____

   c. If Melanie doesn't need to remove money from her bank account, how much money will she have left in her piggy bank? _____

   d. How much money will Melanie have left after Valentine's Day? _____

2. There are 30 students in Mrs. Miller's sixth-grade class. There are 10 girls. Each child puts his/her name on a slip of paper and puts it in a Valentine's box. Two names will be drawn from the box and each child will receive a box of candy.

   a. What is the probability that a boy's name will be drawn from the box first? (Give a fraction, a ratio, and a percentage.) _____

   b. Assuming that the first name selected is the most probable sex, what is the probability that a girl's name will be selected the second time? (Give a fraction, a ratio, and a percentage.)

   _____

3. Philip has a limited supply of red construction paper at home, and he is supposed to cover a shoebox (including the top) and have a one-inch overlap inside the top and bottom of the box. The shoebox is six inches wide, 12 inches long, and 4 inches high. The top is half an inch high.

   a. How much paper (in square inches) will it take to cover the box (outer surfaces and overlap area)? _____

   b. Philip has 4 sheets (8 ½" x 11") of red construction paper. Does he have enough to cover the box? _____

   c. If so, how much extra paper does he have? _____

   d. If not, how much more paper does he need? _____

Valentine Word Search

```
E O V L A R V L E N I T N E L A V P
M L O M O O N L I G H T F E A S A C
U V O M L M W A D F R B N U C T R U
S A A E L A R D V A E T R A R F R P
I N V L V N F B E F I B D Y L I O D
C L R A E C Y H E N E N R O D G W O
C U O O L E T D E F I A W U Y N O P
C V P V S E R E N A D E F O A T A U
L E A Y E L A A D A R F E B R R U C
R D T W D I P U C S A T B A R R Y P
E I S E H T E E W S C A D R O P E I
R E N I T N I L A V P E R T Y O R D
```

arrow	flowers	party
candy	gift	red
card	heart	romance
Cupid	love	serenade
doily	moonlight	sweetheart
February	music	valentine

Decode this Valentine message!

Each letter below stands for a different letter in the alphabet. For example, in this puzzle, every time you see the letter **A** you should write the letter **D** above it.

```
___ ____ ____ _____ ____ _____
C P H U  Z O A  E J S L U  B O D P H  U I Z S J O E

_____ ___ _____ ____ _____
G Z S A U  Z O A  G Z O A H  X J V I  V I B J S

_____ ___ _____ __
K S J B O A U  Z O A  K Z N J L H  P O
              ,
_____ __ ___
W Z L B O V J O B U  A Z H
```

Valentine's Day Activities

Hink Pinks

Hink Pinks are pairs of rhyming words. Next to the clues below, the number of syllables in each word in the answer is shown in parentheses. The first one is done for you.

1. vital-organ store (1, 1) _____heart mart_____

2. blemished valentine (1, 1) _____

3. fine sweets (2, 2) _____

4. dumb matchmaker (2, 2) _____

5. hilarious sweetheart (2, 2) _____

6. romantic-music procession (3, 2) _____

"Valentine" Words

Use the letters in the word "Valentine" to make words consisting of two or more letters each. Place the words in the appropriate columns. Then add your total scores. (You may use the letters only as often as they appear in the word "Valentine." For example, *a* may be used only once in each word.) Do not use abbreviations or proper nouns.

2 letters (1 point)	3 letters (2 points)	4 letters (3 points)	5+ letters (4 points)

Easter Bunnies

Six bunnies recently got together in the forest for a Bunny Convention to discuss their Easter routes and procedures for Easter morning. They sat in a circle surrounded by beautiful spring flowers and counted out colored Easter eggs for each delivery. The bunnies were Peter Rabbit, Flopsy, Mopsy, The Velveteen Rabbit, Cottontail, and Funny Bunny.

One of the bunnies was lazy, one very busy, one constantly munched on carrots, one had droopy ears, one was a superwhiz (this one tried to talk the others into using a computer to determine routes and procedures), and one had really bucked teeth. Decide which characteristic describes each one.

Clues:

1. The bunny with bucked teeth sat at the top of the circle, directly opposite Cottontail.

2. The carrot muncher sat to the right of Cottontail and annoyed him with his constant munching.

3. Flopsy sat between the busy bunny and the bunny with bucked teeth.

4. The lazy bunny sat between the carrot muncher and the Velveteen Rabbit.

5. The busy bunny sat between Flopsy and the bunny who is a superwhiz; Peter Rabbit sat between Funny Bunny and Cottontail.

6. Mopsy sat between the bunny with droopy ears and Cottontail.

7. Funny Bunny was too lazy to count eggs, so the others had to count out his share.

Easter Traditions

England, France, Italy, and Spain have their own word for Easter. They also have certain traditions and customs associated with Easter. One such tradition involves "clipping" a church, which means that everyone joins hands around the outside of the church. Match each country with its word for Easter and its tradition or belief concerning Easter.

Clues:

1. At Pasqua time, Easter cakes are baked in the shape of rabbits.

2. Romans do not wash feet ceremoniously at Easter; nor do they dance to lively music and watch bullfights.

3. The countries located on the European mainland do not refer to the holiday as "Easter."

4. In the country known for its great Notre Dame Cathedral, mothers tell their children that Easter chimes bring eggs. Legend has it that the bells fly to Rome until Easter and drop eggs on the way back for boys and girls to find.

5. The Spanish watch bullfights and dance to lively music in their Pascua celebration.

	Name				Tradition			
	Paques	Easter	Pascua	Pasqua	clipped church	chimes	Easter cakes	dances
England								
France								
Italy								
Spain								

Easter Symbols

Some of the most common Easter symbols are the cross, rabbits, eggs, and lights. These symbols are recognized in many different countries. Use the clues to match groups of people to the Easter symbols they observe.

Clues:

1. The country in which the Sphinx resides thought rabbits were symbolic of birth and new life.

2. Bonfires are not involved in the Easter celebrations of the people from the country where the Olympics originated.

3. One of the groups of people whose homeland is not in Europe believed that Earth hatched from a giant egg.

4. The people of the countries that border the Mediterranean Sea did not believe that Earth had hatched from a giant egg that represented new life.

Symbol

	cross	rabbits	eggs	bonfires
Greeks				
Northern and Central Europeans				
Persians				
Egyptians				

Easter Word Search

```
R A B B I T B E L E C R B E L E C M
Y N N U B B A R A H G T V G V L W U
L E E E T R A D I T I O N S C R Y N
I G G G W B G M A B B I T O H B E D
A S E E I C E L E B R A T I O N A A
T P G T A S L G A P B T E R C A N Y
N S A H E C R O S S O G I H O R D S
O N U S S K U E T N S G I B L N S O
T N U N T N S G E H E M E G A O S S
T R S U D E I A R B E G E C T R O R
O Y D A R S L O B M Y S G R E T R C
C R Y S I T A S U N D A Y S C R S S
```

basket	cross	pastels
bunny	dye	rabbit
candy	Easter	spring
celebration	eggs	Sunday
chimes	hunt	symbols
chocolate	new clothes	traditions
cottontail		

Decode this Easter message!

Each letter below stands for a different letter in the alphabet. For example, in this puzzle, every time you see the letter **M** you should write the letter **E** above it.

```
_ _ _ _ _ _ _ _   _ _ _ _ _   _ _ _   _ _ _ _ _
E A Q H F X M Z   M Z S N G   M U U   A O Z L D

_ _ _   _ _ _   _ _ _ _ _ _ _ _   _ _ _ _   _ _ _ _
R Z F   L A M   D O X V X Q D M D   L A M G   J Q Z F

_ _   _ _ _ _ _ _   _ _ _ _ _ _ _   _ _   _ _ _ _ _ _
Q Z   L A M Q X   K R D T M L D   N Z   M R D L M X

_ _ _ _ _ _ _ .
Y N X Z Q Z U
```

Easter Activities

Hink Pinks

The following hink pinks are pairs of rhyming words that relate to Easter. The numbers in parentheses tell how many syllables are in each word.

1. naked rabbit (1, 1) _____

2. seasonal spree (1, 1) _____

3. holiday food indulger (2, 2) _____

4. hilarious rabbit (2, 2) _____

5. Easter-egg holder seal (2, 2) _____

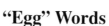

"Egg" Words

Each definition below defines an "egg" word. For example, "precise" defines *eggsact* (exact). Find "egg" words that fit the following definitions.

1. to increase or enlarge something to an abnormal degree _____

2. a test or trial of something _____

3. to praise or glorify _____

4. to do better or greater than others _____

5. to give and receive similar things _____

6. to perform or carry out something_____

7. to drain of power or tire out_____

8. to increase in size _____

9. to breathe out _____

10. a short trip _____

Easter Activities *(cont.)*

"Easter" Words

Write as many words as you can, using the letters in the word "Easter." (If two *e*s are present, your words may have two *e*s, etc. Do not use proper nouns or abbreviations.)

4 letters (1 point)	5 letters (2 points)

Decode This Quotation

The letters in column one will be placed in the blank squares in column one. The letters in column two will be placed in the blank squares in column two, etc. Words are separated by black spaces. It is easy to decode the quotation by determining the short words (one to three letters) first. As letters are used, mark through them at the bottom so that the remaining letters will make it easier to decode the rest of the quotation.

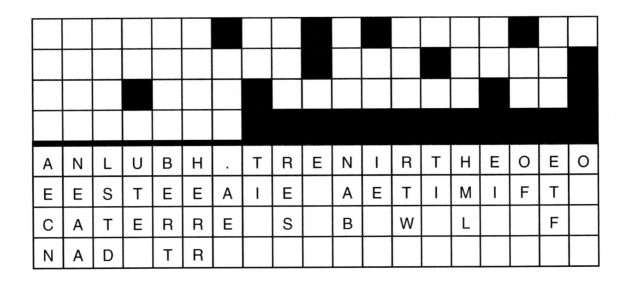

Easter Bunny Math

Six Easter bunnies distributed 10,000 Easter eggs to 500 children on Easter morning. Read the information below, then complete the table below and answer the questions at the bottom of the page.

	# of Eggs	% of Eggs	Fractional Part (reduce)
Peter Rabbit			
Flopsy			
Mopsy			
Velveteen			
Cottontail			
Funny Bunny			
Totals			

Clues:

1. Peter Rabbit delivered the largest percent of the eggs. He delivered 3000 eggs.

2. Flopsy and Funny Bunny delivered the same number of eggs; their combined total was the same as Peter Rabbit's total.

3. The Velveteen Rabbit delivered the least amount of eggs, only $\frac{1}{20}$ of the total. This was half the amount distributed by Mopsy.

4. Cottontail delivered the second highest amount of eggs.

Questions

1. Each child received the same number of eggs. How many eggs did each child receive? _____

2. Each rabbit delivered eggs to a certain number of children. Beside the name of each rabbit, write the number of children to whom she/he delivered eggs.

   a. Peter Rabbit _____   d. Velveteen _____

   b. Flopsy_____   e. Cottontail _____

   c. Mopsy _____   f. Funny Bunny _____

Patriotic Holidays

Five of our nationally observed holidays are Memorial Day (last Monday in May), Independence Day (July 4), Labor Day (first Monday in September), Veterans Day (November 11), and Columbus Day (second Monday in October). These holidays are known by other names, some of which are days celebrated in other countries on the same dates as their American counterparts. Use the following clues to match the two names for each holiday.

Clues:

1. The day that marks the anniversary of America's birthdate is neither Veterans Day nor Columbus Day.

2. The holiday that honors American veterans who fought or lost their lives in wars is not known as the Eight-Hour Day.

3. The Spanish holiday, translated "Day of the Roses," honors the Hispanic heritage of the Latin-American people. The American counterpart of this holiday was named after an explorer for Spain.

4. The two holidays that are celebrated on the same dates every year are neither the Eight-Hour Day nor Decoration Day.

5. Armistice Day and the Eight-Hour Day are celebrated in the fall season of the year.

Holidays' Other Names

	Eight-Hour Day	Armistice Day	U.S. Birthday	Day of the Roses	Decoration Day
Memorial Day					
Independence Day					
Labor Day					
Veterans Day					
Columbus Day					

Presidents

◆ George Washington was the first president of the United States. He was from the state of Virginia and resided in beautiful Mt. Vernon.

◆ Thomas Jefferson was the third president of the United States. He was from the state of Virginia and built his beautiful home, Monticello, there.

◆ Andrew Jackson was the seventh president of the United States. He was born in South Carolina, but he retired to his beautiful Hermitage in Nashville, Tennessee.

◆ Abraham Lincoln was the 16th president of the United States. He was born in Kentucky, but he later moved to Indiana.

Please match these presidents with their nicknames, their wives, and the wars in which they participated.

Clues:

1. The two earliest presidents had wives with the same first name, came from the same state, and were key figures in the same war.

2. Rachel Donelson Robards was still married to Captain Robards when she married "Old Hickory," though she thought she was divorced. Her husband fought in a war that took place in the early 19th century.

3. The most recent of these presidents participated in the American Civil War, and he was not known as the "Father of Our Country."

4. The "Sage of Monticello," also referred to as the "Man of the People," was a lawyer, inventor, architect, draftsman of the Declaration of Independence, and a patriot of the American Revolution.

5. Martha Skelton was not married to the "Father of Our Country," nor did her husband fight in the War of 1812.

Presidents	Nicknames				Wives				Wars			
	Man of the People	Honest Abe	Father of Our Country	Old Hickory	Martha Skelton	Mary Todd	Rachel Robards	Martha Custis	Civil War	War of 1812	Revolutionary War	Revolutionary War
George Washington												
Thomas Jefferson												
Andrew Jackson												
Abraham Lincoln												

Patriotic Word Search

```
M W A S H I D E M O C R A C Y E I K
M A R T I N L U T H E R K I N G N E
E S I I T D A L I W K E N N T K D N
L H T M L D N L O C J R A G L I E N
A I A E A E P H O C G A N R E Y P O
I N O M K E N N E D Y R C T V A E S
R G S O D E E R F G T O A K E D N R
S T A R S A N D S T R I P E S R D E
O O L I N C O L N L U A A V O O E F
N N E A F R E E D O M M N L O B N F
A N I L K N A R F L A G A T R A C E
J N O I T U T I T S N O C N I L E J
```

Adams
Constitution
democracy
Eisenhower
flag

Franklin
freedom
Grant
independence
Jackson

Jefferson
Kennedy
Labor Day
Lincoln
Martin Luther King

memorial
Roosevelt
stars and stripes
Truman
Washington

Decode this patriotic message!

Each letter below stands for a different letter in the alphabet. For example, in this puzzle, every time you see the letter **G,** you should write the letter **A** above it.

_ _ _ _ _   _ _ _ _   _ _ _   _ _ _ _   _ _ _ _ _ _ _ _
H R B C B   R G P B   X B B V   Z G V Q   G Z B C L O G V

_ _ _ _ _ _ _ _   _ _ _   _ _ _ _   _ _ _ _ _ _   _ _ _
M G H C L K H A   E R K   R G P B   D K N I R H   D K C

_ _ _ _ _   _ _ _,   _ _ _   _ _ _ _   _ _ _   _ _ _
Y L P B T   D K C,   G V T   T L B T   D K C   K N C

_ _ _ _ _ _ _ .
D C B B T K Z

Quotations by Famous Presidents

Decode each of the following quotations made by a famous president. Then discuss what you think each president meant by his quote.

A Quotation by Franklin D. Roosevelt

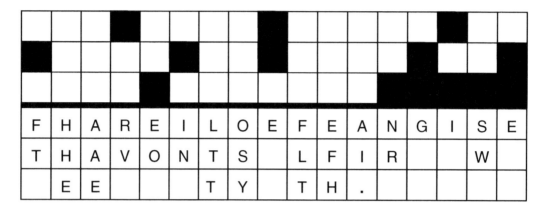

A Quotation by Harry S. Truman

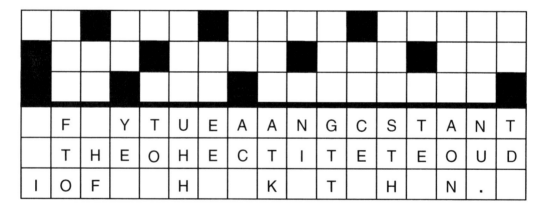

A Quotation by John F. Kennedy

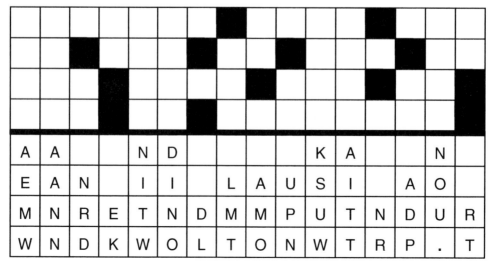

Columbus Day

Christopher Columbus was born in Genoa, Italy, in 1451. He wanted to make a voyage in search of a westward route to Asia by sea. Columbus accepted Marco Polo's mistaken location of Japan and Ptolemy's underestimation of the circumference of the earth and his overestimation of the size of Eurasia. Columbus believed Japan was about 300 miles west of Portugal—a distance he thought he could sail in existing vessels.

After seven years of persuasion, Queen Isabella I of Castille finally gave her support for Columbus's first voyage in search of Asia.

Read the clues below to determine some of the places Columbus visited and discovered and some of the special conditions of each of his four voyages.

Clues:

1. On the first voyage, Columbus left the port of Palos, Spain, on August 3, 1492, with the Niña, Pinta, and Santa Maria.
2. Columbus discovered and circumnavigated Jamaica on his second voyage, but he was not marooned on the island during this trip; nor did he discover South America on that voyage.
3. In July 1498, Columbus landed on Trinidad with six ships. The next day he reached the mainland and discovered South America. He then returned to Santo Domingo (which had been colonized on an earlier voyage), and he and his brother were arrested and sent back to Spain in chains. This was not the last voyage.
4. On one of his voyages, Columbus landed at Martinique and sailed to Santo Domingo, but he wasn't allowed to land because of earlier events on the island. Later in this voyage, Columbus lost his ship and became marooned on the island of Jamaica for one year before he was rescued and returned to Spain.
5. After the fourth voyage, Columbus returned to Spain without greatness or honor at court. He died "thinking" he had reached Asia. The greatness of Columbus lies in the fact that he found the West Indies, returned to Europe, and sailed back to the West Indies many times, even though he made many navigational errors. As a result of his discovery, the New World became part of the European world.

	Conditions				Places Visited			
	6 ships	3 ships	marooned in Jamaica	17 ships	Bahamas	Natividad, Santo Domingo, Jamaica	Trinidad and South America	Martinique
1st Voyage								
2nd Voyage								
3rd Voyage								
4th Voyage								

Martin Luther King, Jr.'s Birthday

Martin Luther King, Jr. was born in the South, in Atlanta, Georgia. He was a very bright student, and he received a doctorate in philosophy. He became a minister and a leader in the Civil Rights Movement. He studied the life and teachings of Mahatma Gandhi, and he accepted the doctrine of nonviolent civil disobedience.

Dr. King was a great leader, and he is the person most responsible for galvanizing the movement to rid the United States of legal racial discrimination. In 1983, Martin Luther King, Jr.'s birthday was declared a federal holiday.

Use this information and the clues below to determine what events took place in certain cities during specific years.

Clues:

1. Martin Luther King, Jr. wrote his first book, *Stride Toward Freedom*, in 1958, before becoming co-pastor of the Ebenezer Baptist Church and president of the Southern Christian Leadership Conference (S.C.L.C.) in Atlanta, Georgia.

2. Martin Luther King, Jr. received a doctorate in philosophy from Boston University in 1955.

3. On December 1, 1955, Rosa Parks defied the ordinance concerning segregated seating on city buses. Later that year, King, Ralph Abernathy, and Edward Nixon led a bus boycott in Montgomery, Alabama. This was eight years before King delivered his famous speech, known as "I Have a Dream," in the U.S. capital.

4. In 1964, Dr. King was chosen as the first black to receive *Time* magazine's "Man of the Year" award. Later that year, he received the Nobel Peace Prize. This was prior to his multiracial poor peoples' march on Washington, D.C., to demand an end to all forms of discrimination and to support the funding of a $12 billion Economic Bill of Rights.

5. On April 4, 1968, King flew to a Southern city (although it was not the city of his birth) to assist striking sanitation workers. There, he was assassinated by James Earl Ray.

Year	City						Event					
	Washington, D.C.	Washington, D.C.	Montgomery, AL	Memphis, TN	Atlanta, GA	Atlanta, GA	Became President of the S.C.L.C.	Bus Boycott	"I Have a Dream"	Economic Bill of Rights	Assisted Striking Sanitation Worker	Birth
1929												
1955												
1960												
1963												
1968												
1968												

Answer Key

page 5

Hink Pinks

1. ghost boast
2. ghoul's tools
3. fat cat
4. fright night
5. bat's hat

Hinky Pinkies

1. witch's britches
2. hobblin' goblin
3. vampire's campfire
4. mummy's rummy
5. bumpkin's pumpkins
6. dandy candy

Hinkity Pinkities

1. skeleton gelatin
2. Dracula's scapulas

page 6

Bobby—money; Bridget—chocolate; Pam—lollipop; Tyler—candy corn

page 7

England—apples, bobbing for apples; Wales—stones, predicting death; Ireland—jack-o'-lanterns, begging for food; United States—pumpkins, trick-or-treating; Scotland—torches, driving away evil spirits

page 8

1. 50 bat tongues

   35 cat tails

   375 goblin toenails
2. 500
3. 606
4. 300; 600; 600
5. 500
6. South Swamp = 8 hours;

   North Swamp = 4 hours

page 9

clockwise, starting from the head of the table:
Dena, The Great Pumpkin; Sarah, Cinderella; Laura, vampire; Mark, Frankenstein; Sean, ghost; Philip, mummy

page 10

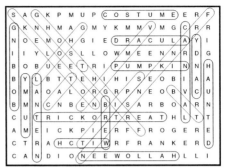

Message: Salem, Massachusetts, is a town in America associated with witches.

page 11

Jeff—ham; Tara—corn; Susie—turkey; Lynne—pumpkin pie; Laura—sweet yams; Kyle—dressing

page 12

Lincoln—1st declared official day, last Thursday in November; Sarah Hale—promoted National Thanksgiving Day, National Thanksgiving; Congress—declared legal federal holiday, 4th Thursday in November; Washington—issued general proclamation, November 26th; Roosevelt—helped business, next-to-last Thursday in November

page 13

clockwise, starting from the head of the table:
Ralph, pie; Mary, dressing; Johnny, potatoes; Susie, rolls; Bill, corn; Ann, green beans; Jeffrey, turkey; Angie, ham

page 14

Hink Pinks

1. fowl howl
2. ham jam
3. buy pie
4. maize craze
5. slim Pilgrim
6. Mayflower power

"Thanksgiving" Words

Accept reasonable answers. Possibilities include the following:

4-letter words: ants, gain, gnat, hint, king, knit, sank, shag, shin, sing, sink, skin, skit, snag, tank, tans, task, thin, vast, etc.

5-letter words: aging, gains, giant, gnash, gnats, hints, kings, knits, shank, sting, stink, thank, thing, think, vista, visit, etc.

Answer Key *(cont.)*

page 14 *(cont)*

6-letter words: giants, giving, hating, hiking, inking, saving, skiing, thanks, things, thinks, etc.

7-letter words: shaking, sinking, skating, staving, thanking, thinking, etc.

page 15

Message: The first Thanksgiving took place over three days. The Pilgrims and the Indians celebrated together.

page 16

1. (⅕ x 8) + (⅒ x 10) = 2 ⅗ pounds
2. $3.25
3. a. 18 cups   f. 4.5 cups
   b. 6 eggs   g. 18 slices
   c. 4 cups   h. 3 tablespoons
   d. 6 tablespoons   i. ¾ cup
   e. 6 egg whites
4. a. $57.60   d. $7.80
   b. $5.76   e. $24.00
   c. $62.40

page 17

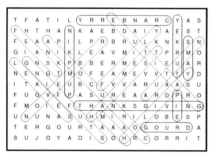

Message: Thanksgiving Day is a time when many Americans gather with their family and count their blessings.

page 18

Santa Claus—orange juice, Blitzen; Mrs. Claus—hot tea, Donner; DePendent Claus—soda, Cupid; Mr. Frostbite—milk, Rudolph; Mrs. Frostbite—hot chocolate, Comet

page 19

Russia—S. Rozhdestvom Khristovym, spider web; Italy—Buon Natale, capitone; France—Joyeux Noel, shoes; Norway—Gledelig Jul, Christmas pudding; Spain—Felices Pascuas, Jota

page 20

from left to right: Richard, stereo; Sarah, skateboard; Tim, skates; Nick, sneakers; Ashli, baseball glove; Jeni, video game

page 21

1. 36,525
2. 1 A.M. Christmas Day
3. a. 464   b. 468   c. 484
4. Cupid = 80 m.p.h.; Rudolph = 240 m.p.h.;
   Blitzen = 360 m.p.h.
5. 2 years ago = 160 lbs.; 1 year ago = 160 lbs.;
   this year = 240 lbs.

page 22

Message: Christmas is an exciting time for children—a time filled with joy and excitement!

page 23

Hink Pinks

1. Claus floss   4. jolly holly
2. thrift gift   5. carol apparel
3. free tree

"Christmas" Words

Accept reasonable answers. Possibilities include the following:

3-letter words: act, air, arm, art, car, cat, ham, him, his, hat, hit, its, mat, ram, rat, rim, sat, sir, sit, etc.

4-letter words: cash, cart, cast, cats, chat, rams, rats, hair, harm, math, mass, mast, mist, mats, miss, char, star, stir, mash, trim, tram, mart, mach, etc.

5-letter words: amiss, march, masts, trams, trims, stars, match, hairs, charm, chars, chasm, chats, mirth, harms, etc.

6-letter words: smarts, charms, charts, chairs, chasms, starch, stairs, smirch, etc.

Answer Key *(cont.)*

pages 24 and 25

1. Rome, Italy
2. Suez
3. Red Sea
4. Abidjan
5. Madagascar
6. South Korea
7. 10:00 p.m.
8. India
9. Himalaya
10. 3° N 103° E
11. Australia
12. Perth
13. northeast
14. 6 time zones
15. Rocky
16. Ottawa
17. Bogota
18. Andes
19. Rio de Janeiro

page 26

John—Jennifer, candy; Sean—Cathy, funny valentine; Chris—Erin, romantic valentine; Steve—Monica, spider; Jason—Lisa, sticker

page 27

England—Valentine Buns; Denmark—gaekkebrevs; Italy—Valentine Feast; Canada—Valentine Cards

page 28

1st—Ben and Jennifer; 2nd—Ted and Kelly; 3rd—Shawn and Heather; 4th—Jason and Julie; 5th—John and Angie

page 29

1. a. $19.60   b. no
   c. yes—$5.40   d. $105.40
2. a. 2/3; 2:1; 67%
   b. 10/29; 10:19; 34.5%
3. a. 396 sq. inches   c. no answer required
   b. no   d. 22 square inches

page 30

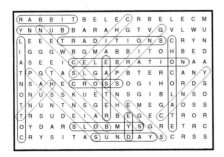

Message: Boys and girls enjoy sharing cards and candy with their friends and family on Valentine's Day.

page 31

Hink Pinks

1. heart mart
2. marred (or scarred) card
3. dandy candy
4. stupid Cupid
5. funny honey
6. serenade parade

"Valentine" Words

Accept reasonable answers. Possibilities include the following:

2-letter words: an, at, in, it

3-letter words: ail, ale, ant, eat, eel, eve, inn, lea, let, lit, net, nit, tan, tea, tee, tie, tin, van, vat, vie, etc.

4-letter words: late, lent, lint, live, neat, tail, tale, teal, tine, vale, veal, vent, vile, vine, etc.

5-letter words: alien, alive, entail, invent, linen, liven, valet, vital, etc.

page 32

clockwise: Velveteen Rabbit, bucked teeth; Funny Bunny, lazy; Peter Rabbit, carrot muncher; Cottontail, superwhiz; Mopsy, busy; Flopsy, droopy ears

page 33

England—Easter, clipped church; France—Paques, chimes; Italy—Pasqua, Easter cakes; Spain—Pascua, dances

page 34

Greeks—cross; Northern and Central Europeans—bonfires; Persians—eggs; Egyptians—rabbits

page 35

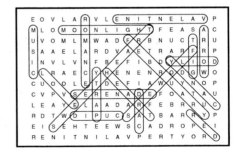

Message: Children enjoy egg hunts and the surprises they find in their baskets on Easter morning.

Answer Key (cont.)

page 36

Hink Pinks

1. bare hare
2. spring fling
3. Easter feaster
4. funny bunny
5. basket gasket

"Egg" Words

1. exaggerate
2. examine
3. exalt
4. excel
5. exchange
6. execute
7. exhaust
8. expand
9. exhale
10. excursion

page 37

4-letter words: arts, east, eats, rate, rats, rest, sate, sear, seat, seer, star, tear, teas, tees, tree, etc.

5-letter words: rates, stare, steer, tears, tease, terse, trees, etc.

Quotation: Easter is a time to celebrate new life and the rebirth of nature.

page 38

Peter Rabbit = 3000; 30%; 3/10

Flopsy = 1500; 15%; 3/20

Mopsy = 1000; 10%; 1/10

Velveteen = 500; 5%; 1/20

Cottontail = 2500; 25%; 1/4

Funny Bunny = 1500; 15%; 3/20

Totals = 10,000; 100%; 100/100 = 1

1. 20 eggs
2. a. Peter Rabbit = 150
   b. Flopsy = 75
   c. Mopsy = 50
   d. Velveteen = 25
   e. Cottontail = 125
   f. Funny Bunny = 75

page 39

Memorial Day—Decoration Day
Independence Day—U.S. Birthday
Labor Day—Eight-Hour Day
Veteran's Day—Armistice Day
Columbus Day—Day of the Roses

page 40

George Washington—Father of Our Country, Martha Custis, Revolutionary War;
Thomas Jefferson—Man of the People, Martha Skelton, Revolutionary War;
Andrew Jackson—Old Hickory, Rachel Robards, War of 1812;
Abraham Lincoln—Honest Abe, Mary Todd, Civil War

page 41

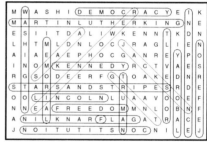

Message: There have been many American patriots who have fought for, lived for, and died for our freedom.

page 42

Roosevelt Quote: "The only thing we have to fear is fear itself."

Truman Quote: "If you can't stand the heat, get out of the kitchen."

Kennedy Quote: "Mankind must put an end to war or war will put an end to mankind."

page 43

1st Voyage—3 ships, Bahamas; 2nd Voyage—17 ships, Natividad, Santo Domingo, Jamaica; 3rd Voyage—6 ships, Trinidad and South America; 4th Voyage—marooned in Jamaica, Martinique

page 44

1929—Atlanta, Birth; 1955—Montgomery, Bus Boycott; 1960—Atlanta, President of Southern Christian Leadership Council; 1963—Washington, "I Have a Dream"; 1968—Washington, Economic Bill of Rights; 1968—Memphis, Assisted Striking Sanitation Workers